THE #1 Dad BOOK

A list of titles by James Patterson appears at the back of this book

THE #1 Dad BOOK

JAMES PATTERSON

CENTURY

UK | USA | Canada | Ireland | Australia
India | New Zealand | South Africa

Century is part of the Penguin Random House group of companies whose addresses can be found at global.penguinrandomhouse.com

Penguin Random House UK,
One Embassy Gardens, 8 Viaduct Gardens, London SW11 7BW

penguin.co.uk
global.penguinrandomhouse.com

First published 2025
002

Printed and bound in Great Britain by Clays Ltd, Elcograf S.p.A.

The authorised representative in the EEA is Penguin Random House Ireland, Morrison Chambers, 32 Nassau Street, Dublin D02 YH68

A CIP catalogue record for this book is available from the British Library

ISBN: 978–1–529–96269–7

Penguin Random House is committed to a sustainable future for our business, our readers and our planet. This book is made from Forest Stewardship Council® certified paper.

THE #1 Dad BOOK

The Most Important Thing You'll Ever Do Is Be the Best Dad You Can Be

Hey, dad.

(Or soon-to-be dad.)

I get it.

You're busy as a beaver in flood times. Busy as popcorn in a skillet.

You're distracted.

You're under pressures people don't always understand.

You don't have time for…well, lots of things you'd like to have time for.

You're frustrated at times.

Just the other day, you couldn't find the car keys, or your wallet, or the TV remote.

Or all of the above.

Occasionally, you can be a knucklehead.

That's okay.

This batshit crazy world isn't making things any easier.

It's like the title of that old show from Broadway: *Stop the World—I Want to Get Off.*

You can't get off this not-so-merry-go-round, though.

But you do love your kids (or kid) more than anything.

You want them to have really good lives.

You're doing the best you can.

But you know what? *You can do better.*

Yeah, you can.

These pages can help.

It'll be quick...and mostly painless.

And it *will* make you a better dad.

Even if just two, or three, or five of these ideas work for you.

You'll be a better dad. Maybe a whole lot better.

And that'll be a good thing for everybody you care about.

Especially your kids.

I did the homework, so you don't have to do as much. I talked to lots of experts, and lots of dads, and lots of experts who are also dads. I read everything I could. Then I wrote and rewrote this book.

The pro-football coach Bill Parcells once said, "You are what your record says you are."

Your kids are *your* record.

So, turn the page, dad.

You're in.

You just made a big commitment.

One hour.

Operating Instructions (For This Book, Not Your Kids)

Don't be afraid to mark up these pages with a sawed-off pencil or a pen subversively leaking ink.

Or use crayons. Or colored pencils. Go wild. Underline or highlight anything that makes sense to you.

This is going to work, big guy.

It's like a writer friend of mine told me, "Once a really good idea gets inside your head, it's impossible to get it out."

And there are some good ideas here, I promise!

Put a big fat check mark next to the ones that sound right to you—those are the things you *know* you can do to get better as a pop.

On the flip side, some of these tips might feel all wrong to you. Or to your partner. They might even seem stupid. Or simplistic. Or too politically correct. Or too politically incorrect.

Cross out anything and everything you *don't* agree with! Be aggressive with those ~~cross outs~~!

The job here—success—is to get better. Just making this one-hour commitment is a good start.

When you think about it, becoming a better dad is like anything else you've learned to get better at. You've probably figured out how to get better at some sport. Maybe you've learned to cook. Or at least grill. You've learned how to get better at your job.

You practiced. You concentrated. And you got better. Maybe a lot better.

So, you've done this before.

The ESPN host Dick Schaap said there were only two kinds of teams.

The ones filled with people trying to make the world dumber. And the ones filled with people trying to smarten it up.

Be a smarten-upper.

You can even make up dumb words like *smarten-upper.*

"I realized what fatherhood really meant when our first child, our son, was born and he was unable to breathe. I felt a surge of anguish and terror and grief because it was so wrong that he would have never been fully alive before he could simply disappear. That's something like the awakening I think every father feels at some time in his life. Our son recovered, grew up, and he's an absolutely great guy."

—BILL, JOURNALIST; ONE DAUGHTER, ONE SON

Here's to New Dads—and Old Vets

Maybe you're a newbie. Or maybe you're becoming a dad again. Whatever kind of dad you are, congrats! You're part of a sacred brotherhood. And a fatherhood. A very long line of dads. At times, that can be very comforting.

You're not alone.

First, you need to know this: After the baby is born, everybody will be mostly fussing over mom and the baby, not you. That's natural. It's totally fair.

Pregnancy is an unbelievably tough gig. You have no idea. Me neither.

And babies have their own adorable ways of demanding attention.

But what about the dad?

After the baby comes, dads need some hugs too. Dads need the occasional "attaboy."

Because pregnancy is hard for the dad too.

There, I said it. Out loud.

Mom, if you're reading this, go ahead and throw this very nice book (that you probably bought) at the nearest wall.

But show dad some compassion. He's not as smart as you.

And everything just changed for him too.

❝

"Like so much between fathers and sons, playing catch was tender and tense at the same time."

—DONALD HALL, POET; ONE DAUGHTER, ONE SON

Name Calling

Okay, so what are you going to name your new human? That's a very good topic for your babymoon. (Some couples take a trip before the baby is born. It's called a babymoon. Didn't take one myself, but it sounds like a cool idea.)

This is one of your first dad jobs. And it's a big one. Talk it over with your partner. Sleep on it. And don't take it lightly.

Here's a tip from a wise, helpful person: Before your baby is born, practice calling out the names you like at the dinner table a few dozen times. At the top of your lungs.

Which names sound best?

Which names are easiest to pronounce?

Which names get old really fast?

Remember, whatever name you choose, you're going to be calling it out many thousands of times over the next eighteen years. Make sure it rolls off your tongue.

Don't saddle your kid with a name that seems funny, or cute, or clever in the moment. Remember, it's not your name. It's the name your kid has to live with. Every day. For the rest of his or her life.

And not to get morbid, but someday it will be etched on a tombstone. *Here lies Mildred.* Or Ethel. Or Dick. Or Danger. Yes, some parents have named their child Danger.

Of course, that's not to say that kids can't make good with an unusual name.

Elvis made it work somehow.

So did Eldrick—though he's better known as Tiger.

Hopefully, so will Apple, a girl named after a very delicious fruit by her movie-star mom, Gwyneth Paltrow, and rock-star dad, Chris Martin.

My wife's dad's name was *Orville Berthold* Solie.

He decided he wanted to be called O.B.

Smart man.

O.B. became a very, very good dad.

He named his baby girl *Susan.*

"What brings us together is our love of music. I'm from Jamaica, and we love hip-hop. Sometimes my daughter and I will go out on our own 'date' and that's when we talk about *everything*. At dinner, I'm not Daddy. I'm her friend. Sometimes she says...'Forget you're my dad...We're going to talk like friends.' Becoming a dad taught me what love is. I never really knew anything about love until I became a dad."

—GESLEY, RESTAURANT MANAGER; ONE DAUGHTER

Things Are About to Get Messy

I know your time is valuable. I respect that. The one-hour clock is ticking.

We might as well get right into it.

Between your baby's birth and the end of toilet training, you'll be changing about eight thousand diapers. A lot of those diapers will be somewhere between foul and disgusting.

Get used to it.

Embrace the poop.

Laugh at the poop.

Talk to the poop.

"Wow! How could so much poop come out of such a small person? This is impressive. Must be some kind of world record."

Above all, don't put off dealing with the poop. Or the pee. You may not remember, but diaper rash really sucks. If it was your dirty underwear, you'd change it in a hurry, right?

It's not that hard. Just a little gross. Gross is no big deal.

So, roll up your sleeves, hold your breath, do your job.

Same goes for feeding time and bath time.

You're going to get sticky. You're going to get wet. So what? Dive right in.

Volunteer for service.

And remember this when you're at the supermarket. Seriously, don't mess up here. Baby wipes are essential for the health of your baby's behind. And for your mental health. And your partner's.

You can never have too many. Don't scrimp. Buy in bulk.

A lot of dad stuff is doing little things like that.

That's why it's easy to get better.

One mess at a time.

"The nature of impending fatherhood is that you are doing something that you're unqualified to do."

—JOHN GREEN, AUTHOR; ONE SON, ONE DAUGHTER

“

"Our son is three. Fatherhood? It's the best feeling in the world. Puts a smile on my face early in the morning. Gives me energy when I'm tired. I want our boy to do whatever makes him happy. But there's such a thing as the family business. If your father is a carpenter, you probably know a little bit about wood. If your father is a plumber, you know something about pipes. I've been involved with pro baseball all my life. If he wants to play baseball, great. If not, also great."

—CRAIG, BASEBALL SCOUT; ONE SON

Not a Hugger? You Will Be in a Minute

If there's one thing a lot of kid experts agree on, it's that human touch is life itself for babies. Remember, the little one just spent nine months *inside another body.* He or she craves contact.

Hold those little babies as much as you can.

Press them against your heart. They love to hear it thumping.

Hug them while they're awake. Hug them while they're sleeping.

They can't get enough of you.

Okay, sometimes they'll slime your favorite shirt. Or pants. Or even your ballcap. But that's a small price to pay.

And hugging isn't just for babies.

I have a good friend who raised a couple of football-playing boys. One Saturday night, the boys got up from the table after we all had dinner. They were about to walk out the front door when my friend called out to them: "Where do you two think you're going?"

The boys, big-time football players, came back and gave their dad a hug.

That scene taught me a lesson that I never forgot. More important, I've lived by it ever since.

Our son got a hug every morning when we dropped him off at school. We couldn't have cared less what the other kids thought. He felt the same way we did.

He's grown up now. But whenever he comes home, he still gets a hug.

He always will.

The author George Saunders said something that's been guiding me for the last couple of years.

It's this: "My time here is short—what can I do the most beautifully?"

One of the most beautiful things you can do is become a better father.

Starting with a hug.

"From the time our kids were very young, we would say, 'Let's do a big hug!' We'd put our arms around each other in a circle, draw in close, very close, and start saying in a quiet voice, 'AHHHH,' with eventual crescendos, *'AHHHH,'* until it was loud enough that we were all giggling. We still do it to this day."

—Mark, doctor; two daughters

"Be very loving, and by *loving*, I mean not just caring for your child—touching them, carrying them when they're little, hugging them, telling them you love them."

—JIM, CONSULTANT; THREE DAUGHTERS

"My father was not a hugger...not an affection guy...He showed his love in other ways...working hard...giving up everything...My kids hug...They know that I love them."

—DOUG, TEACHER; FOUR SONS

You're One Big, Beautiful Noise

By this point in your life, you've probably figured out that not everybody is in love with the sound of your voice.

But guess what? Your baby is.

It's a fact. Your voice is one of the greatest things he or she has ever heard.

So, sing to your baby. Even if you can't hold a tune.

Babies love rock 'n' roll. They love rap. They even like opera.

Talk to them before they can speak.

Once they start to talk, they'll have a lot of very smart questions.

Know why?

Because everything in the infinite number of universes is new to them.

So, try to answer their questions. Talk back in their alien tongue.

Teach them words from *your* alien language. Try not to teach them the f-word. Unless you want them using it in preschool.

Some studies show a father's vocabulary has a stronger effect on kids' language development than a mom's.

Okay, let's say it's a fifty-fifty thing, but play your part.

There will be days when you wish the terrible twos were far, far behind you.

Maybe put a check mark next to this one.

The ones and twos and threes will be over in the blink of an eye.

Gone girl. Gone boy.

Then what? Then you get old, dad. That happens in the blink of an eye too.

So, talk to your kids. Early and often.

And don't ever stop.

"I have a four-year-old and a teenager. It's like, get ready to have all your plans destroyed. The four-year-old talks a lot. He's going to Christian school. One day I told him to clean his room. He said to me, 'Jesus is upset, and he is going to come and put me in the Thinking Chair.' The Thinking Chair is what they call a time-out at the Christian school. I tried not to laugh, but he was so serious about it."

—ISRAEL, FILMMAKER; ONE SON, ONE STEPSON

If You Read Nothing Else, Read This

Read to your kids.

You.

Read.

It doesn't take much time to make a big difference.

Reading to your kids helps boost their brainpower.

It gives them new words and new ways of putting them together.

Think about this: Kids whose parents read to them daily are exposed to almost *three hundred thousand more words* before kindergarten than kids whose parents don't read to them.

That's more words than the first three Harry Potter books combined.

A pretty good head start going into school, right?

Reading to your kids exposes them to big emotions in stories and shows them that those feelings are normal.

(It's also a great time for you to ask questions like

"Have you ever felt like that?" or "What do you think would make Pooh feel better?")

Read to your kids until they're four or five.

Then flip things around. Let them read to you.

And don't just pick books that *you* think are good.

Find books that *they* think are good.

Let them see books in your house.

Here are some pretty cool books to read to your kids when they're little.

Be Glad Your Dad...(Is Not an Octopus!) by Matthew Logelin and Sara Jensen, illustrated by Jared Chapman

It's always a bonus when kids get to learn something new and interesting while reading. This book gives kids lots of reasons to be glad their dad is who he is, and ends on fun facts about the animal dads featured in the story.

I Am Every Good Thing by Derrick Barnes, illustrated by Gordon C. James

This empowering ode to all the energy, goodness, and wonder in kids is also an ode to Black boyhood, and provides great affirmations to remind kids of their limitless potential.

The Book with No Pictures by B. J. Novak

A great read aloud for dads who love to be silly and make their kids laugh…and who don't mind saying "boo-boo butt" out loud.

Because I'm Your Dad by Ahmet Zappa, illustrated by Dan Santat

Nothing compares to the unconditional love a parent has for their child, and Ahmet Zappa (Frank Zappa's son) captures that perfectly here. The book is also silly and fun, making it another great read aloud.

Houdini and Me by Dan Gutman

If you're looking for a novel to read together with an older kid, you can't go wrong picking a book by Dan Gutman. This one stars an eleven-year-old who is contacted by someone claiming to be Harry Houdini. There is great Houdini trivia, and plenty of action and twists to keep kids and adults turning the pages.

"It is easier to build strong children than to repair broken men."

—FREDERICK DOUGLASS, ABOLITIONIST LEADER; THREE SONS, TWO DAUGHTERS

Be Consistent, Consistently

This is a biggie: Consistency builds trust. And trust is the foundation for just about everything that matters.

Be consistently fair with your kids.

Because your kids need to trust you.

They need to know you have their back.

You need to know they have your back.

Listening is incredibly important for building trust.

So is patience. And repetition.

Yep, *repetition.*

And never be afraid to say these three words to your kids, or your partner:

I. Was. Wrong.

Consistent doesn't mean boring. Here's a way to look at it.

Be consistently surprising. Good surprises take a little thought. Good surprises take a little planning.

Your kids might not always gush over your surprises at the time. Sometimes you'll wonder if they appreciate them at all.

Guess what? Years later, when you least expect it, they'll tell you how much those surprises meant.

It will happen. I promise.

Don't be surprised.

"I know a lot of single men and women who don't want to have children. Because it's work. Because it will change their lifestyle. But it's worth it. It's totally worth it. You don't know that until you hold your own child in your arms."

—JIM, CONSULTANT; THREE DAUGHTERS

What's Your Story, Dude?

Here's another easy thing we can all do as dads.

Tell your kids your story. Make that your *stories.* Plural.

What do you value most? What's really important to you? What can't you live without? What *can* you live without?

Don't go on and on. Don't bore them to tears. Just tell them who you are, and more important, tell them what you stand for.

And then, let them tell you *their* stories.

Listen to your kids. Find out who they are. At their core.

If they're really not sure yet, if they're still struggling with it, help them to figure it out. It's hard. Remember how hard it was for you as a kid?

If the kids are already teens, or preteens, don't wait. Do it right away.

The idea is not to change your kids into who you are.

Or who you always wanted to be.

It's to help them discover who *they* are. Deep down inside.

Of course, once you open yourself up, your kids might also want to give you some free advice about yourself. That's a good thing.

It means they're interested. It means they care. And you'll be surprised at how much they've noticed about you.

Listen to their ideas about how you can get better. Don't be afraid to ask for help. That might be worth a check mark. In fact, I'll say it again:

Don't be afraid to ask for help.

Especially from your kids.

Nobody knows you better.

Here's a hard truth for me to tell: I think if I'd written this book before I had our son, I would've been a better dad.

❝

"When our son was born, that week, I started a journal of messages to him. I wrote my last entry just before he graduated from high school. I gave it to him after graduation, and he didn't even know that I had it. He started reading it at our dinner table, and we were crying and laughing at the same time."

—JEFF, EDUCATOR; ONE SON, ONE DAUGHTER

Find Yourself Some Dad Buds

How many hours do you spend talking to other guys about work stuff? About fantasy football? About politics? About that balky sump pump in your basement?

Maybe, once in a while, try talking about dad stuff.

About what your kids are going through.

About what *you're* going through.

About your partner, and how they're doing.

Not every dad will be into it. Some of us need to play everything really close to the vest. No sharing.

But if you find a few who are willing to talk, you'll be amazed at how much you have in common, how much you can learn from one another, and how good it feels to share the load.

By the way, moms have been talking to one another like this for thousands of years. Maybe millions.

It's worked out pretty well.

❝

"I've got a friend with four girls. Three of them are teenagers. He and I talk about our kids at least once a week. We've become best friends because of those talks. Our kids are close too. And our wives."

—NEAL, HOUSEPAINTER; TWO DAUGHTERS, ONE SON

Your Presence
Is Required

Here's one of my trade secrets: When I'm writing a novel, I sometimes scrawl a note to myself at the top of a page that says, "Be there." It reminds me that I need to put the reader in the scene so that they'll really feel it.

The same goes for being a dad.

Let's be honest. There are lots of distractions in life. The Internet. Zoom calls with in-laws. Night shifts. Netflix. The NFL Draft.

There will be times when you can only give your kids part of your attention. But whenever you can, as much as you can, *focus*!

It's not just being around, although that's a big part of it. It's paying attention, setting other thoughts aside, and really being present. There are some woo-woo terms for this. *Intention. Mindfulness.* But what it comes down to is:

When you're with your kids, *be there.*

Have you ever seen little kids on a school stage lighting up when they spot their parents in the audience? It's like they're witnessing a miracle.

Now you're the miracle.

You might not be able to be at every recital, every birthday party, and every game.

But be at as many as you can.

It matters.

Sure, somebody else can shoot video of a game or birthday.

But it's only *live* once.

Years later, your kids will not remember what song they sang, what flavor cake they had, or whether they won or lost that third match of the season.

But they'll remember if you were there.

"Show up. You can't miss anything.
You gotta be there for them.
Your job can't get in the way, and it will.
When they tell you, 'It's okay, you don't
have to be there,' don't listen to them.
Just show up."

—BOB, TEACHER; TWO DAUGHTERS

Old School

vs.

New School

vs.

You School

This is something a lot of dads struggle with. You don't have to be an old-school dad. Or a new-school dad.

Maybe the right thing is to take the best of both schools.

You do you.

No matter what you decide, good habits are hugely important.

What are some good habits that you can pass on to the kids?

And some bad habits that you can improve on—so that those bad habits *don't* get passed on?

You could make a list.

Unless that sounds stupid to you.

Then *don't* make a list.

But just in case you want to:

GOOD HABITS:

____

____

____

____

BAD HABITS:

____

____

____

____

I'll start.

Here's a good habit of mine. At least I think it's a good habit. I write every day. Seven days a week. And the thing is, I don't feel like I work for a living, I play for a living.

So that's probably a good habit.

Do I have bad habits? Yep. I eat too many hamburgers and drink too much soda.

And that's all you're getting out of me.

"I had a great father. He busted his ass. He was a blue-collar teamster truck driver for thirty-eight years. Back when I was a kid, I was playing hockey. My brother was on the same team. Our father was at the game. There was a guy on the other team really giving it to my brother. A dirty player. So, I nailed him good. During the fight, I was cursing. After the game, my father came up to me, and I could tell he was mad. He said he wasn't upset because I defended my brother. He said, 'Did you have to use such foul language?' To this day, my dad is my role model. Maybe now more than ever."

—Joe, coach; two sons

Those Oldies but Goodies

Here's some good news, dad. A rare win-win for you and the kids.

If your parents or those of your partner are around, you're blessed. Maybe twice blessed.

And so are your children.

Just build a relationship between your kids and your parents. Go with the flow. It will make you a better dad.

Most grandparents love their grandchildren. And grandchildren love their grandparents. So, you're starting from a position of strength.

Grandparents are from another generation. That can be a real plus. They experienced a very different world, and used life's tools that are almost unrecognizable today. "What is a typewriter?" "Black-and-white TV?" "Station wagons?" "You walked to school in the snow with no shoes?"

The positive side is that they can teach your kids a little history.

And give them some context about your family.

Maybe even an origin story or two.

They have stories to tell. Sometimes over and over.

But these are stories that will stay with your kids for the rest of their lives and maybe be passed on to your grandchildren.

They also knew relatives who aren't around anymore, but they're still part of your kids' DNA.

Some survived tragedy.

Some triumphed over adversity.

Some did small, everyday things that carry big lessons.

Some were just funny as hell.

Some of you might be saying, "I didn't exactly get along that well with my parents."

Well, get out of the way. This is about your kids. Your parents are probably different now, and the relationship between grandparents and grandchildren is definitely different than the one between you and your mom and dad.

Bonus!

Always remember this—grandparents are a great resource for free childcare and lots of cool presents.

"A few things in life are better than advertised, and one of them is being a grandparent. Grandchildren are the greatest gift our daughter and son-in-law could have possibly given to us. Time with our grandchildren is precious for my wife and me."

—BOB, ATTORNEY; ONE DAUGHTER, THREE GRANDKIDS

The Incredible Power of No

Okay, remember that I'm just talking here. We're spending an hour together.

So, just for a minute, let's talk about saying no.

To your kids.

It can be a hard thing. But a good thing. A *necessary* thing.

People who know about this stuff say that dads who establish boundaries from the start are less likely to have kids with behavioral issues later.

And here's the secret that kids will never tell you: They actually *crave* boundaries. Boundaries help them feel safe.

It's not always easy. Kids are geniuses, diabolically clever about getting their way. And they will definitely test your limits. That's part of growing up.

But don't cave in when they throw temper tantrums or beg, or plead with those big, expressive eyes of theirs.

Don't reward bad behavior.

That's one of the most common mistakes we all make as parents.

Do not reward bad behavior.

And try to avoid anything that smacks of punishment for punishment's sake. Just because you're mad at them in the moment, don't take it out on them. You're the adult. You're the one they need to trust.

There have to be some rules in the house, right? Hopefully, not too many rules. And the rules need to be understood by everybody. They need to be fair. This isn't boot camp.

Here's one rule that fits all: When it's called for, you should absolutely say, "You can't talk to me or your mom like that."

That's a big no.

And the same goes for you when you're talking to your kids.

Words hurt.

Kindness counts.

And it goes both ways.

"Kids remember everything. Everything! Just about everything you've ever said, everything you've done. Things that you've forgotten, they remind you about twenty years later."

—JOHN, JOURNALIST; THREE DAUGHTERS

“We were four boys.
We loved being around my dad.
We used to watch everything he did.
We would sit down and watch him eat.
And try to chew like him. The way he walked. I said, ‘That’s the guy I want to be when I grow up.’ I was a screwup. I probably shouldn’t be in the police. I was hanging around with the wrong people. But I learned from my father. He never, ever raised his hand, or even his voice. He’d sit down and talk to you, and you’d feel like you got your butt whipped. But he never touched any of us.”

—Carlos, deputy police chief; one daughter

Let's Take It Outside

Most child psychologists—and most experienced dads—will back me up on this:

Never argue in front of the kids.

Especially *about* the kids.

They're watching. They're listening. They're learning.

The only time you should be raising your voice to your partner is when you're laughing your head off.

Or singing off-key.

Whatever issues or disagreements you're having, the two of you can talk it through later, one-on-one. No kids allowed.

If it can't wait, maybe go into the garage. Or out into the backyard. Or onto that nice little patio on the roof of your apartment building.

Whatever it takes, keep meanness out of your house.

You want meanness in your house even less than you want rodents.

Unless you just got suckered into having a pet hamster.

Rookie mistake.

When kids see parents argue, they get anxious. And when partners take opposite sides, kids get confused. And confusion breaks down trust.

Seeing parents argue is an opportunity that some kids will use to play you against each other. (They're clever that way.)

If your kids try to play the "but mom said" game, your response is simple.

"Well, let's go ask mom about that right now."

To get to mom, they've got to go through you, dad.

And vice versa.

Arguments between adult partners are natural and healthy.

But when the kids are around: United You Stand.

"They see everything.
They hear everything...
They don't need a list of things they need to be. They just need an example of what to be. They need you. Being an example shouldn't be 'Oh, I did this,' or 'You should do that.' It's more subtle. Kids read the room instantly."

—TERENCE, ATTORNEY; TWO SONS, ONE DAUGHTER

Love Is in the Air (Or It Should Be)

Kids benefit from seeing their parents respecting each other and being affectionate with each other.

A little parental PDA can show them what a healthy, loving relationship looks like.

So let them see you holding hands.

Let them see you hug.

Let them see you kiss.

Let them hear you say, "I love you."

If you do it often enough, they'll learn not to chirp *ewww!* every time.

Now, some dads will say, "I'm not an 'I love you' kind of guy."

Says who? Who passed that law? Your dad? Your dad's dad?

You can be an "I love you" guy.

You can change. At least a little.

You'll be a better man for it.

Saying "I love you" is not a sign of weakness.
It's a sign of strength.
Now go ahead. Say "I love you."
Was that so hard?
If it was, say it again.
Okay, *I'll* say it. "I love you, man."

"

"My youngest has a rare disease that affects his cognitive ability. He decided to be one of the speakers at his graduation. He's so shy and quiet that we questioned his decision before he went ahead with it. He gave this incredibly humble speech of gratitude. It was all about his school, his teachers, and the other kids. The part that really got us is that he broke down three times while he was speaking. My son doesn't cry. It was a beautiful thing to see my child had grown into someone so incredibly strong."

—SCOTT, TEACHER; THREE SONS

My Bad

Guys, let's face it. We screw up a lot. I know I do. Sometimes, royally.

But here's the silver lining. That means we can be really, really good at teaching kids about resilience.

And how to confront challenges.

And deal with mistakes.

And *own* them.

Life isn't always fair. You already know that. But it's important that your kids learn it too. You don't have to be overly negative, or pessimistic, just realistic.

Muhammad Ali used to say, "There's nothing wrong with getting knocked down, as long as you get right back up."

Don't be afraid to discuss tough topics with your kids. They can take it.

Help them make good decisions.

Get them ready for the real world.

It's not getting any easier out there. To be honest, it seems to be getting harder every year.

You don't need to scare them. Just prepare them.

"We had this discussion a lot.
Sometimes you have to let them sink
to learn how to swim.
Don't be their life vest, not all the time—
you have to let them sink."

—STEVE, PHOTOGRAPHER; TWO DAUGHTERS

Laugh It Off

With kids, a sense of humor is necessary for survival.

Yours and theirs.

When the going gets tough, sometimes the tough have to get funny. Sometimes the best thing you can do is laugh.

Be a goofball sometimes.

Adam Sandler meets Chris Rock. That's you.

Did you hear the one about the three stages for becoming a dad? First, you believe in Santa Claus. Then you don't believe in Santa Claus. Then you *are* Santa Claus.

Not that funny? So what? Try another joke.

Laugh at the situation.

Laugh at the problem.

Laugh at yourself. Hell, everybody else does.

Laughing releases tension.

It floods your brain with endorphins.

It's a bonding experience. The best possible kind.

The family that laughs together stays together.

"The thing about our meals together—at home, at Mickey D's, wherever—there're always laughs. Everybody thinks they're the funniest ever. But I know I'm the funniest. That's a joke."

—TED, CONSTRUCTION WORKER; TWO SONS, TWO DAUGHTERS

"My daughter is really cool. Really smart. I'm kind of the clown in her world. It's always, 'Dad, oh Dad.' She thinks it's funny the way I dress, or the dance moves I make, or the fact that I listen to her music. The best advice I got from another dad is, 'It only gets better; you're going to get all this incredible enrichment. Hang on tight.'"

—ANDREW, ASSISTANT MANAGER; ONE SON, ONE DAUGHTER

The Good,
the Bad,
and the Boring

There's no getting around it.

No matter how much you adore your kids, there will be times when dadhood is drudgery.

I'm not talking about changing diapers. Or rocking your little baby to sleep. We've covered all that.

I'm talking about later.

Like when your kid wants to watch the same Disney movie for the hundredth time.

Or when you have to pretend to love playing a video game that involves elves and magic coins.

Or when you have to be the Helping Dad at preschool.

That's hard time, my friend.

There will be days when you're convinced your brain is turning to mush. When you think you're losing your edge. When you feel like you've been reduced to a camp counselor, a babysitter, or a chauffeur. Or all three at once.

There will be times when you'll mutter—softly, to yourself—that you can't wait for the day to end.

But trust me on this—

There will come a time, not too far in the future, when you would pay a million dollars to have just one of those days back.

"My wife and I are both lucky.
We had good, loving parents guiding us.
So, we sort of inherited our parenting
skills. If you're lucky like that,
then emulate your parents."

—STEVE, PHOTOGRAPHER; TWO DAUGHTERS

"The process of living or working with children is demanding and exhausting. It requires heart, intelligence, and stamina. When we don't live up to our own expectations—and we won't always—let's be as kind to ourselves as we are to our youngsters. If our children deserve a thousand chances, and then one more, let's give ourselves a thousand chances—and then two more."

—ADELE FABER AND ELAINE MAZLISH,
HOW TO TALK SO KIDS WILL LISTEN & LISTEN SO KIDS WILL TALK

The Magic of Rituals

Kids crave dependable patterns. Even if they don't know it. Even when they wouldn't admit it.

Schedule regular time with them. Don't just expect it to happen. *Make* it happen.

Be creative. Be a little clever. Be the charming guy you can be when you want to.

If you work from home these days, you have no excuses. Just start a little later once in a while. Or knock off a little early. Or block out some time on your schedule. It's as important as any meeting or deadline.

No. It's *more* important.

If you work in an office or a factory or a hospital or an Amazon warehouse, finding a regular time can be harder. Same for dads who drive trucks or manage farms or travel for a living.

But remember, it doesn't have to be a lot. It just

needs to be something your kids can count on. Something for them to look forward to. Something *consistent.* (See how that keeps coming back?)

Some families already have a lot of traditions. If you do, bring the kids in on them. Give them important roles.

If you don't have a lot of traditions, create some.

One of the simplest traditions starts around the table.

Whenever you can, eat meals as a family.

Some of the best conversations you will ever have will be at the dinner table with your kids.

What you'll remember most is their laughter.

Each one of those laughs is unique.

A thing unto itself.

A thing of beauty.

Definitely worth repeating.

"The most important thing is to get your kids to talk to you. In our house, I had this amnesty kind of thing. We had this white bench in the front yard, and I told the kids...when we're sitting on this bench you can tell me anything and it doesn't leave the bench. I called it the B.T....the Bench Talk. It was a safe spot for me and the kids."

—ERIC, ATTORNEY; TWO DAUGHTERS

The Lesson of the Five Balls

I've always found this useful. I've pretty much lived by it.

Imagine life as a game in which you are juggling five balls in the air.

You name them—work, family, health, friends, and spirit—and you're keeping all of these in the air.

Hopefully, you will soon understand that work is a rubber ball. If you drop it, it will bounce back.

But the other four balls—family, health, friends, and spirit—are made of glass.

If you drop one of these, they will be irrevocably *scuffed, marked, nicked, damaged,* or even *shattered.* They will never be the same.

Once we understand that, maybe, just maybe, we will strive for more balance in our lives.

Tattoo This Behind Your Eyeballs

We're pals now, right?

So, you can take it when I give you some bad news.

Actually, you already know it, or at least you suspect it.

Let me break it to you as gently as I can:

It's time to grow the fuck up.

No more BASE jumping.

No more treks to Burning Man.

No more swimming with sharks.

If you're still smoking, or vaping, or chewing tobacco, now is the time to quit.

Ask yourself if you might be playing sports more often than you should. Like twice a week in your beer league. Followed by beers.

Or golfing both days on the weekend.

A few of my goofball friends, all dads, played in a men's basketball league into their mid-fifties. They had team jerseys that said Nobody Moves, Nobody Gets Hurt.

Unfortunately, they got hurt. A lot. Sprained ankles, broken fingers, dashed egos.

Do your family a favor. Take better care of yourself.

You might still feel like a kid.

But you're not.

You're a dad.

Try to stay off the injured list.

You're
the Man—
Live with It,
Live Up to It

You're (half) in charge of helping your kids take responsibility for their actions. If they did it, they need to own it. They do the crime, they do the time. (Hopefully, no real crimes.)

It starts with helping your kids understand the difference between right and wrong.

Sometimes, there are complicated, deep-rooted reasons why we make mistakes. Why we fail. But at some point, we have to take responsibility for our actions.

Help your kids. They're young. They're mostly innocent. They can be knuckleheads at times. But they do need to understand that actions have consequences.

Kids also need to understand that *character* means doing the right thing.

Even in an empty room, when nobody's watching.

Even if some people are getting away with doing the wrong thing. And they *are*.

Folks doing the wrong thing shouldn't be role models for our kids. But that's the case way too often. Especially on the Internet.

And that's where you come in, dad.

And not with too heavy a hand.

And not too often.

Just enough.

You've got the touch.

❝

"My father was quiet and handsome, an all-American running back in the 1940s. Eventually a football coach. He was also very superstitious. For years my brothers and I wondered why he would never walk in front of a parked car, always behind it. Why would he never wear a seat belt? Why he would whisper what seemed a quick, quiet prayer before driving us around as kids. When I got older, I finally asked him about these silent quirks. He told me as a Navy flier in the Pacific he would pray before bombing runs and tap his St. Christopher's medal. No seat belt? He said too many guys he trained with died, strapped in, trapped in cockpits when their planes crash-landed, as his B-24 did on a remote Japanese island. Why avoid the front of a parked car? He recounted seeing airmen obliterated when they walked right into the invisible, spinning propellers of warplanes parked on hot, noisy flight lines...no doubt a horror he could never unsee. The idiosyncrasies and prayers that my brothers and I often joked about were his private release from experiences he kept to himself...likely for our sake. It wasn't weakness, or odd behavior. It was strength. That was his generation."

—TIM, JOURNALIST; NO KIDS

Be Patient with Your Kids, with Your Partner, with Yourself

Most good things don't happen all at once.

That includes becoming a better dad.

Improve one small thing at a time, then another, and another.

One step at a time.

Rinse and repeat.

Patience is hugely important...

Take a deep breath before you say another word.

Deeper breath.

Go on a walk. Or a run. Or a car ride.

It's like the pissed-off email you don't send. Zip it, pops.

Also, praise your kids.

When they do something good, clap, cheer, go out for pizza at their favorite place. Not *your* favorite place, *their* favorite place.

But keep it real. Not everybody gets a trophy in life. For better or worse, the world doesn't work that way.

If your son or daughter has two left feet, they may not be destined to become a ballet dancer. At least not professionally. But they can still have a blast dancing around the house. Let them be themselves.

On the other hand, don't be afraid to tell the kids about things they're doing that could cause them harm and pain in the world lurking outside your house.

Do it gently.

Try not to be preachy.

(I know. I'm being a little preachy.)

Here's a little trick for giving advice to kids. Because *sometimes, they don't want to hear it from you.*

Maybe start by saying, "I'm sure you've already thought of this..." That usually gets them listening, gets them leaning in.

Another random thought: Clothes don't make the kid. It's not about what they're wearing, it's about who they are. *Inside.*

Teach them to be kind.

Kind kids don't make fun of other kids. Kind kids don't even make fun of their sibs. Not too much anyway.

"A lot of [parenting] is about the example you set for your kids—how you talk to them, how you talk to other people around them, and setting that example of what it means to be kind, polite, grateful, [and] honest."

—Emmy-, Grammy-, Oscar-, and Tony-winning artist John Legend; two sons, two daughters

Dealing with Screenagers

If you were born in the Digital Dark Ages (before 1997), you have no idea what your kids are dealing with today.

The Internet was one thing. Social platforms are a whole different ball game. They're addictive. They're invasive. They're relentless. And they can be truly harmful to your kids' mental health.

Politicians and tech companies keep talking about making social sites safer for kids. But it's mostly just talk.

Meanwhile, these ubiquitous screens with their devious algorithms are taking over young people's lives.

Sorry. That got a little heavy.

So, what can a dad do? Make your kids use a landline?

No Freaking Way.

But you can lay down some laws. (Kindly and consistently, of course.)

No devices at the dinner table, for example. And that includes *your* phone.

Or no screen time when you're together in the car. (But they get to pick the playlist.)

There are even ways to set screen-time limits on your kids' devices. Don't ask me how. Just google it.

You can't monitor your child's social media use 24/7. And kids are very wily at finding work-arounds for restrictions. Even if you're pretty tech-savvy, trust me, the average middle schooler will leave you in the dust.

But if you start to see your kid preferring social media to human contact, or losing sleep because of screen time, take action.

It's dad time.

No,

We Didn't

Forget

About You.

How Could We?

You're Not a Dad...
and That's 100 Percent Okay

What about the guys who aren't dads?

Whether by choice or by circumstances, being a dad isn't for everyone.

Maybe you wanted children, but weren't in the right relationship at the right time.

Maybe you have a medical history that makes having kids challenging, or not possible.

Maybe you just...don't really want to spend all of your time with rug rats.

Perfectly understandable. For a while, I felt that way myself.

It's normal to question taking on a role so challenging, so draining—emotionally and financially—and so all-consuming.

But chances are, there are still plenty of "dad" opportunities for you.

You care about the world, its future, and the kids growing up in it.

Those kids may not be your own sons and daughters, but they need your help.

Everybody needs somebody who...

> ...believes in them.
>
> ...shows them how to get to where they're going.
>
> ...makes them feel seen and heard.

My grandmother was that person for me. She taught me to work hard—with purpose—and to have a hell of a lot of fun doing it.

Her lesson was simple and to the point: "Hungry dogs run faster."

That doesn't mean they run alone.

Sign up. Pitch in. Show what you know. Show your stuff.

It's okay if you don't want to be a full-time dad. You have talent and experience to give.

Give to kids when they're young, and the gifts will last a lifetime:

Kids growing up and getting better jobs.

Kids developing a love for books.

Kids eventually being able to vote and figuring out who they want to vote for.

Kids living good lives.

BE A MENTOR.

You work hard at your job. You've learned a lot about life. Don't keep it to yourself.

Recently, I was invited to speak at a conference on storytelling. The moderator was someone I knew years before. She told some stories about what I was like as a boss. I was touched to hear her use the word *inspiring.* What meant even more was when she pointed to one example I set—writing every day—as a key to her becoming a big-deal boss herself with a job she loves. *She* was inspiring that day.

BE A COACH.

You played sports. You watch sports. You know sports.

Everyone remembers their favorite coach. The one who taught them how to throw a perfect football spiral, or a curve or slider in baseball.

The one who taught them how to lose a game without losing their cool.

Be that guy.

BE AN UNCLE.

If you have a brother or sister with kids, you've got a potentially terrific role to play with your nieces and nephews. You know your brother or sister better than anyone. Their likes, their dislikes. What makes them laugh. What makes them cry. What makes them tick.

You can become just as close with their kids.

Spend time with those nieces and nephews. It doesn't matter whether it's planned or spontaneous.

Play catch.

Play Minecraft.

Find the last piece of a jigsaw puzzle—but let them put it in.

Come to school events.

Take pictures or home movies at graduation.

Cheer them on.

Never forget a birthday.

Take them on wild, mostly safe adventures.

Ask them for *their* opinion.

Tell them *yours.*

And one day when they have kids, you can be their favorite *great*-uncle.

Repeat

After Me:

"I'm a Good Guy,

I'm a Good Guy,

I'm a Good Guy..."

Sometimes, we just need to hear ourselves say it.

Deep down, most dads are sensitive. And vulnerable. And more than a little stubborn. Maybe we never entirely stop being little boys.

It's okay to talk about your feelings with the kids. It just might help you understand yourself a little better too.

The truth is, if you don't love and respect yourself, it's going to be hard to pass on love to your kids.

So look at yourself in the mirror every morning, first thing, and tell yourself you're okay. Every morning.

If it isn't morning right now, go to a mirror and tell yourself you're okay anyway.

You're a good guy, dad.

Just don't get carried away with yourself.

Here are some things worth thinking over:

Living healthier.

Whatever that means for your family.

Take walks together.

Take hikes together.

Climb mountains together.

Your kids are worth it.

You're worth it.

Walk away from abusing alcohol or drugs, and even cigarettes and vaping.

You might think that you can't do it, but you can do a whole lot better.

That's all we're talking about in this hour that we're spending together.

Doing better.

Not being perfect.

Just better.

More Good Stuff

The rewards of being a better dad never stop, they just keep coming.

Kids with a strong attachment to their dads feel less anxious, less alone, less lost at sea.

We want that, right?

Well, we're in charge. At least partly in charge.

Think about your kids as much as you can. While you're shaving. When you're driving to work. During your lunch break. On your evening run. Or when you're just sitting in the old easy chair.

The rewards make every little, or big, sacrifice worth it. Ten times over.

Fathers can show daughters that they deserve respect from males. That's a huge thing you can do.

Good fathers have kids with higher self-esteem. That's a big one too.

They raise kids to be curious about the world.

They meet their kids' friends.

And if you do that, even some of that, chances are pretty good your kids will be your friends for life.

Our son now lives far away in big, bad New York City. But he calls a couple times a week.

I know Susan and I didn't do everything right. But we did a lot of little things okay.

And we can get better.

"My eight-year-old daughter, out of the blue, announced one day that she was definitely going to be an artist. Some parents would say that's a crazy idea. No! Let your kids run with it. Our daughter has worked in museums all over the world and ended up with a job she loves at Christie's."

—JIM, CONSULTANT; THREE DAUGHTERS

Better Dads Make Better Partners

Better dads step up.

Better dads are full partners.

Better dads do their share of the dirty work.

Better dads give their partners a break once in a while.

Some dads told me they go to sleep holding hands with their partner. Sounds like a great, sane way to end the day.

Especially a tough day.

After all, you're in this together.

You're raising the precious babies you brought into the world.

Nothing can beat that. Nothing will ever be more important.

And that's a really good place to stop.

Our hour's up.

Let's have a beer. Or a soda. Or a cold lemonade.

You are now officially off the clock.

Overtime

Want to know more about how to be a better dad? These experts have been studying it for a lot longer than I have.

Here are some great books if you want to do a deeper dive.

Presence: Bringing Your Boldest Self to Your Biggest Challenges by Amy Cuddy

Manifest power and avoid the negative feedback loop: That's the strategic advice found in this book—based on social psychologist Amy Cuddy's famous TED Talk on "power poses"—about showing your best self to your entire family.

There Are Dads Way Worse Than You: Unimpeachable Evidence of Your Excellence as a Father by Glenn Boozan

This might look like a picture book, but it's definitely for grown-ups. If you're like me and into pop culture and history, you'll especially appreciate the references. Read this one when you've had a tough parenting day—you'll get a laugh and some reassurance.

The New One: Painfully True Stories from a Reluctant Dad by Mike Birbiglia, with poems by J. Hope Stein

In life and parenting, it helps to have a sense of humor. This comedian's take on becoming a dad shows the good, bad, and funny sides of parenthood.

Things My Son Needs to Know About the World by Fredrik Backman

You might know Fredrik Backman from *A Man Called Ove* or *Anxious People*. This is something completely different, a series of lists and essays that show how fatherhood can be daunting, challenging, or rewarding—sometimes all three at once.

Why Fathers Cry at Night: A Memoir in Love Poems, Letters, Recipes, and Remembrances by Kwame Alexander

Kwame Alexander is a talented poet and author (together we wrote a book for kids, *Becoming Muhammad Ali*). He takes an emotional, introspective turn here to tell a story of love, especially his love for his daughters, through poems, letters, recipes, and essays.

Let’s Go to the Videotape

If just two, or three, or five of these ideas work for you—you'll be a better dad, and that's one hour very well spent.

1. Be consistently fair. Trust really is built on consistency. And trust is everything.
2. Be a listener. Listen to your kids. Listen to your partner. Listen to yourself.
3. Learn how to say *I. Was. Wrong.* Just in case it ever happens.
4. Don't be afraid to say, "I love you." Say it now. Loud and proud.
5. Be a hugger. Hey, give yourself a hug every once in a while.
6. Tell your kids your story. Listen to theirs.
7. Read to your kids. Let them see books in your house.

8. Have your kids' backs. One day, they'll have yours.
9. Teach your kids to be responsible for their actions. And to be kind. That's the sweet spot—kindness.
10. Learn the value of the firm no.
11. Change the stinky diapers, get wet at bath time, sing the little darlings to sleep.
12. Be an all-world role model for your kids.
13. Don't argue in front of the kids.
14. Grow the fuck up. It's time.
15. Eat as a family. And eat healthy. Most of the time anyway.
16. Be a better dad and you'll be a better partner.
17. Find other dads to talk it out with.

It's been a real honor talking to you.

Extra Credit

Before I go, here's one more thought that might help.

Make a list of the things in your life that really piss you off.

The worst of the worst.

Stuff that makes your blood boil.

Makes you grit your teeth.

Now. Cross out everything you can't do anything about.

Just let it go.

Then maybe try to fix what's left on your list.

All the best to you. It's been an honor.

ACKNOWLEDGMENTS

A lot of dads, and moms, and a few folks with no kids helped with this book. I want to single out just a few: Mark Ormson, Matt Eversmann, Dr. Brigid Balboni, Isabelle Morris, Bob Barnett, Ned Mahoney, Mike Lupica, Tim Malloy, John Keresty, Joe Denyeau, Bill Robinson, Ned Rust, Steve Bowen, Charles H. Patterson, Susan Solie Patterson.

ABOUT THE AUTHOR

James Patterson is one of the best-known and biggest-selling writers of all time. Among his creations are some of the world's most popular series, including Alex Cross, the Women's Murder Club, Michael Bennett and the Private novels. He has written many other number one bestsellers including collaborations with President Bill Clinton, Dolly Parton and Michael Crichton, stand-alone thrillers and non-fiction. James has donated millions in grants to independent bookshops and has been the most borrowed adult author in UK libraries for the past fourteen years in a row. He lives in Florida with his family.

Also By James Patterson

ALEX CROSS NOVELS

Along Came a Spider • Kiss the Girls • Jack and Jill • Cat and Mouse • Pop Goes the Weasel • Roses are Red • Violets are Blue • Four Blind Mice • The Big Bad Wolf • London Bridges • Mary, Mary • Cross • Double Cross • Cross Country • Alex Cross's Trial (*with Richard DiLallo*) • I, Alex Cross • Cross Fire • Kill Alex Cross • Merry Christmas, Alex Cross • Alex Cross, Run • Cross My Heart • Hope to Die • Cross Justice • Cross the Line • The People vs. Alex Cross • Target: Alex Cross • Criss Cross • Deadly Cross • Fear No Evil • Triple Cross • Alex Cross Must Die • The House of Cross

THE WOMEN'S MURDER CLUB SERIES

1st to Die (*with Andrew Gross*) • 2nd Chance (*with Andrew Gross*) • 3rd Degree (*with Andrew Gross*) • 4th of July (*with Maxine Paetro*) • The 5th Horseman (*with Maxine Paetro*) • The 6th Target (*with Maxine Paetro*) • 7th Heaven (*with Maxine Paetro*) • 8th Confession (*with Maxine Paetro*) • 9th Judgement (*with Maxine Paetro*) • 10th Anniversary (*with Maxine Paetro*) • 11th Hour (*with Maxine Paetro*) • 12th of Never (*with Maxine Paetro*) • Unlucky 13 (*with Maxine Paetro*) • 14th Deadly Sin (*with Maxine Paetro*) • 15th Affair (*with Maxine Paetro*) • 16th Seduction (*with Maxine Paetro*) • 17th Suspect (*with Maxine Paetro*) • 18th Abduction (*with Maxine Paetro*) • 19th Christmas (*with Maxine Paetro*) • 20th Victim (*with Maxine Paetro*) • 21st Birthday (*with Maxine Paetro*) • 22 Seconds (*with Maxine Paetro*) • 23rd Midnight (*with Maxine Paetro*) • The 24th Hour (*with Maxine Paetro*) • 25 Alive (*with Maxine Paetro*)

DETECTIVE MICHAEL BENNETT SERIES

Step on a Crack (*with Michael Ledwidge*) • Run for Your Life (*with Michael Ledwidge*) • Worst Case (*with Michael Ledwidge*) • Tick Tock (*with Michael Ledwidge*) • I, Michael Bennett (*with Michael Ledwidge*) • Gone (*with Michael Ledwidge*) • Burn (*with Michael Ledwidge*) • Alert (*with Michael Ledwidge*) • Bullseye (*with Michael Ledwidge*) • Haunted (*with James O. Born*) • Ambush (*with James O. Born*) • Blindside (*with James O. Born*) • The Russian (*with James O. Born*) • Shattered (*with James O. Born*) • Obsessed (*with James O. Born*) • Crosshairs (*with James O. Born*) • Paranoia (*with James O. Born*)

PRIVATE NOVELS

Private (*with Maxine Paetro*) • Private London (*with Mark Pearson*) • Private Games (*with Mark Sullivan*) • Private: No. 1 Suspect (*with Maxine Paetro*) • Private Berlin (*with Mark Sullivan*) • Private Down Under (*with Michael White*) • Private L.A. (*with Mark Sullivan*) • Private India (*with Ashwin Sanghi*) • Private Vegas (*with Maxine Paetro*) • Private Sydney (*with Kathryn Fox*) • Private Paris (*with Mark Sullivan*) • The Games (*with Mark Sullivan*) • Private Delhi (*with Ashwin Sanghi*) • Private Princess (*with Rees Jones*) • Private Moscow (*with Adam Hamdy*) • Private Rogue (*with Adam Hamdy*) • Private Beijing (*with Adam Hamdy*) • Private Rome (*with Adam Hamdy*) • Private Monaco (*with Adam Hamdy*)

NYPD RED SERIES

NYPD Red (*with Marshall Karp*) • NYPD Red 2 (*with Marshall Karp*) • NYPD Red 3 (*with Marshall Karp*) • NYPD Red 4 (*with Marshall Karp*) • NYPD Red 5 (*with Marshall Karp*) • NYPD Red 6 (*with Marshall Karp*)

DETECTIVE HARRIET BLUE SERIES

Never Never (*with Candice Fox*) • Fifty Fifty (*with Candice Fox*) • Liar Liar (*with Candice Fox*) • Hush Hush (*with Candice Fox*)

INSTINCT SERIES

Instinct (*with Howard Roughan, previously published as* Murder Games) • Killer Instinct (*with Howard Roughan*) • Steal (*with Howard Roughan*)

THE BLACK BOOK SERIES

The Black Book (*with David Ellis*) • The Red Book (*with David Ellis*) • Escape (*with David Ellis*)

TEXAS RANGER SERIES

Texas Ranger (*with Andrew Bourelle*) • Texas Outlaw (*with Andrew Bourelle*) • The Texas Murders (*with Andrew Bourelle*)

STAND-ALONE THRILLERS

The Thomas Berryman Number • Hide and Seek • Black Market • The Midnight Club • Honeymoon (*with Howard Roughan*) • Sail (*with Howard Roughan*) • Swimsuit (*with Maxine Paetro*) • Don't Blink (*with Howard Roughan*) • Postcard Killers (*with Liza Marklund*) • Toys (*with Neil McMahon*) • Now You See Her (*with Michael Ledwidge*) • Kill Me If You Can (*with Marshall Karp*) • Guilty Wives (*with David Ellis*) • Zoo (*with Michael Ledwidge*) • Second Honeymoon (*with Howard Roughan*) • Mistress (*with David Ellis*) • Invisible (*with David Ellis*) • Truth or Die (*with Howard Roughan*) • Murder House (*with David Ellis*) • The Store (*with Richard DiLallo*) • The President is Missing (*with Bill Clinton*) • Revenge (*with Andrew Holmes*) • Juror No. 3 (*with Nancy Allen*) • The First Lady (*with Brendan DuBois*) • The Chef (*with*

Max DiLallo) • Out of Sight (*with Brendan DuBois*) • Unsolved (*with David Ellis*) • The Inn (*with Candice Fox*) • Lost (*with James O. Born*) • The Summer House (*with Brendan DuBois*) • 1st Case (*with Chris Tebbetts*) • Cajun Justice (*with Tucker Axum*)• The Midwife Murders (*with Richard DiLallo*) • The Coast-to-Coast Murders (*with J.D. Barker*) • Three Women Disappear (*with Shan Serafin*) • The President's Daughter (*with Bill Clinton*) • The Shadow (*with Brian Sitts*) • The Noise (*with J.D. Barker*) • 2 Sisters Detective Agency (*with Candice Fox*) • Jailhouse Lawyer (*with Nancy Allen*) • The Horsewoman (*with Mike Lupica*) • Run Rose Run (*with Dolly Parton*) • Death of the Black Widow (*with J.D. Barker*) • The Ninth Month (*with Richard DiLallo*) • The Girl in the Castle (*with Emily Raymond*) • Blowback (*with Brendan DuBois*) • The Twelve Topsy-Turvy, Very Messy Days of Christmas (*with Tad Safran*) • The Perfect Assassin (*with Brian Sitts*) • House of Wolves (*with Mike Lupica*) • Countdown (*with Brendan DuBois*) • Cross Down (*with Brendan DuBois*) • Circle of Death (*with Brian Sitts*) • Lion & Lamb (with *Duane Swierczynski*) • 12 Months to Live (*with Mike Lupica*) • Holmes, Margaret and Poe (*with Brian Sitts*) • The No. 1 Lawyer (*with Nancy Allen*) • Eruption (*with Michael Crichton*) • The Murder Inn (*with Candice Fox*) • Confessions of the Dead (*with J.D. Barker*) • 8 Months Left (*with Mike Lupica*) • Lies He Told Me (*with David Ellis*) • Murder Island (*with Brian Sitts*) • Raised By Wolves (*with Emily Raymond*) • Holmes is Missing (*with Brian Sitts*) • 2 Sisters Murder Investigations (*with Candice Fox*)

NON-FICTION

Torn Apart (*with Hal and Cory Friedman*) • The Murder of King Tut (*with Martin Dugard*) • All-American Murder (*with Alex Abramovich and Mike Harvkey*) • The Kennedy Curse (*with Cynthia Fagen*) • The Last Days of John Lennon (*with Casey Sherman and Dave Wedge*) • Walk in My Combat Boots (*with Matt Eversmann and Chris Mooney*) • ER Nurses (*with Matt Eversmann*) • James Patterson by James Patterson: The Stories of My Life • Diana,

William and Harry (*with Chris Mooney*) • American Cops (*with Matt Eversmann*) • What Really Happens in Vegas (*with Mark Seal*) • The Secret Lives of Booksellers and Librarians (*with Matt Eversmann*) • Tiger, Tiger • American Heroes (*with Matt Eversmann*)

MURDER IS FOREVER TRUE CRIME

Murder, Interrupted (*with Alex Abramovich and Christopher Charles*) • Home Sweet Murder (*with Andrew Bourelle and Scott Slaven*) • Murder Beyond the Grave (*with Andrew Bourelle and Christopher Charles*) • Murder Thy Neighbour (*with Andrew Bourelle and Max DiLallo*) • Murder of Innocence (*with Max DiLallo and Andrew Bourelle*) • Till Murder Do Us Part (*with Andrew Bourelle and Max DiLallo*)

COLLECTIONS

Triple Threat (*with Max DiLallo and Andrew Bourelle*) • Kill or Be Killed (*with Maxine Paetro, Rees Jones, Shan Serafin and Emily Raymond*) • The Moores are Missing (*with Loren D. Estleman, Sam Hawken and Ed Chatterton*) • The Family Lawyer (*with Robert Rotstein, Christopher Charles and Rachel Howzell Hall*) • Murder in Paradise (*with Doug Allyn, Connor Hyde and Duane Swierczynski*) • The House Next Door (*with Susan DiLallo, Max DiLallo and Brendan DuBois*) • 13-Minute Murder (*with Shan Serafin, Christopher Farnsworth and Scott Slaven*) • The River Murders (*with James O. Born*) • The Palm Beach Murders (*with James O. Born, Duane Swierczynski and Tim Arnold*) • Paris Detective • 3 Days to Live • 23 ½ Lies (*with Maxine Paetro*)

For more information about James Patterson's novels, visit www.penguin.co.uk.